P9-CDE-748

My Parents Are Getting DIVORCED

WEST GA REG LIB SYS
Neva Lomason
Memorial Library

Other books in the
sunscreen series:

sex explained
honest answers to your questions about
guys & girls, your changing body, and
what really happens during sex

just us girls
secrets to feeling good
about yourself, inside and out

feeling freakish?
how to be comfortable in your own skin

My Parents Are Getting
DIVORCED

how to keep it together when your
mom and dad are splitting up

Florence Cadier with Melissa Daly
illustrated by Claire Gandini

sunscreen

Book series designed by Higashi Glaser Design

Library of Congress Cataloging-in-Publication data has been applied for.

ISBN: 0-8109-9163-2

Text copyright © 2004 Florence Cadier with Melissa Daly
Illustrations copyright © 2003 Claire Gandini

Translated by Jackie Strachan and Jane Moseley, JMS Books, LLP

AMULET

Published in 2004 by Amulet Books
an imprint of Harry N. Abrams, Incorporated
100 Fifth Avenue
New York, NY 10011
www.abramsbooks.com

All rights reserved. No part of the contents of this book may
be reproduced without the written permission of the publisher.

Printed and bound in China.
10 9 8 7 6 5 4 3 2 1

Abrams is a subsidiary of
LA MARTINIÈRE

With special thanks to David H. Levy,
family law specialist in Chicago

contents

phase 3:

THE START OF A NEW LIFE

WILL MY PARENTS SPLIT UP? IS IT MY FAULT? WHAT WILL HAPPEN TO ME? DO I HAVE TO CHOOSE SIDES? ARE WE STILL A FAMILY? DO MY PARENTS STILL LOVE ME?

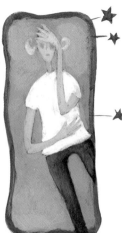

You probably thought divorce was something that only happened to other people. But now it's your parents who are doing the arguing, fighting, and splitting up. Suddenly, you're one of those people divorce is happening to. You're probably feeling disoriented and confused, as if the structure of your daily life is about to collapse. And you have every right to be anxious: the coming months may bring tense moments, hard times, and maybe even harsh legal decisions that affect the whole family. You'll hear people talking about child support, custody, lawyers, and rulings—some of which you may not fully understand, but most of which sound sort of scary, or at best, unpleasant. You might also be feeling angry with your parents for deciding to separate and forcing you to live through the aftermath.

Everyone's situation is slightly different because every relationship is unique. But many of your feelings and questions are shared by thousands of other kids whose parents are getting divorced. In time, things will get better. Once everything has settled down again, you'll still be part of a family—it'll just be a little different and will take some getting used to. And when you do get used to it, you may even be happier with your new and improved family life.

TENSION AT HOME

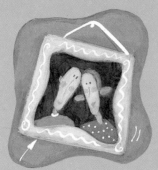

dealing wi

is it all my fault?

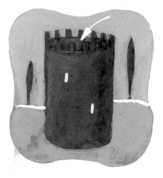

keeping to myself

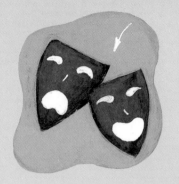

everyone reacts
differently

ARGUMENTS

and other

PROBLEMS

growing up too soon

a weird

atmosphere

Crash! There goes another glass, smashed on the kitchen floor. A bedroom door slams shut violently. The foundations of the house seem to shake, and so do you. Your parents are fighting again. The atmosphere at your house has probably been pretty electric lately. Even the smallest thing—such as someone forgetting to buy milk, or being twenty minutes late for dinner—sparks off another shouting match. Maybe your dad has taken to sleeping on the sofa, or your mom always seems to have meetings that keep her out of the house when your dad is home. Because when they're in the same room together, you could cut the tension with a knife. Sound familiar?

Meanwhile, your parents are trying to convince you to be more patient and more tolerant with your siblings: "Stop bickering . . . you're the oldest . . . let your little brother watch his cartoons . . . you can watch your show when he's in bed." But it's not as if they're setting a great example—they're the ones that need the "getting along" speech! The language they use and the nasty looks they give each other make it all too clear that there are real problems going on between them. This isn't some TV show—it's real life. It's your real life and theirs. Even if nobody has mentioned the word "separation" yet, you can tell that something major is about to happen.

Just living your daily life is becoming more difficult. You might feel trapped between your mom and dad and their problems, and too scared to talk about things like what's going on at school, or with your friends, for fear that some random detail might start another battle. Besides, your parents don't seem to be even remotely interested in what's happening with you anyway, at least not like they used to, before they were so preoccupied all the time. No one would blame you if you started hanging out at your friends' places more often, where it's much more calm and predictable, instead of inviting them over to the madhouse.

If all this rings true for you, it sounds as if the "cold war" has set in at home. The signs vary from family to family. Sometimes the parents start communicating only in formal, unfriendly sentences, such as "Please let me know if you are prepared to pick up Caroline from her dance class." Other parents manage to ignore each other pretty successfully, except when crises come up—like a dinner invitation from mutual friends or a decision about who'll pick the car up from the garage. Aside from these moments when your parents are forced to speak, entire meals may be

spent in total silence—or sprinkled with nasty comments. You may ask your mother's advice, but your father contradicts her. Or you ask permission to stay out late, and one of them plays the "nice parent" and says yes, but the other one says no. Suddenly, you don't know who to listen to. On especially bad nights, when things start escalating out of control, you might even start to get scared that they'll really hurt each other—or you.

It's normal for you to be worried about your parents' fighting and about what will happen if they decide to get a divorce. Breaking up is bad enough when you're a teenager, but it's even harder when it's adults who are married and have children together. Breakups happen when two people can no longer maintain a happy relationship. They may agree that they're just not compatible anymore, or one of them may blame the breakup on the other. But in most breakups, both parents play a part.

bread

how did it happe

Sometimes, adults stop loving each other or just aren't able to get along anymore. It happens. You already knew that. But now it is not just some adults, it's *your* adults! And you never thought it would happen to you. Even if you watched your friends go through it, you probably still felt somehow protected from it. For some reason, it's always really hard to imagine your own parents not liking each other anymore. Yeah, okay, sometimes your brothers and sisters get on your nerves but you wouldn't throw them out just because they were annoying! You've always seen your parents as an inseparable unit, two people who are part of one whole. It's only natural for you to picture your future with both of them at your side. Which can only make you ask yourself . . . what happened?

It could be that living together for several years didn't bring your parents closer together in the way they thought it would. They grew apart instead of growing together, and now they don't have that much in common anymore. They're not in love the way they were at the start, or they may now realize that they never truly were. How could that be? Well, when we're young, life seems a little simpler—agreeing on what movie to see on Friday night and which jokes in it are the funniest goes a long way. But as we get older, there are more important things to deal with, and sometimes that means more things to disagree on. For instance, maybe your mother loves going out and being involved in a million community projects, but your father wishes she spent more quiet time at home. Or maybe your dad likes to make all the financial decisions, but your mom wishes he'd consult with her before he spends a ton of money. Or maybe one of them likes to talk for hours to work every problem out, but the other prefers to take some time apart, sleep on things, and let them work themselves out on their own.

Conflicts such as these may seem like small things, but when you face them every day, they can start to feel really overwhelming.

it's so hard to

There are many possible reasons why your parents have grown apart, and some of them are really personal, intimate, and hard for outsiders to understand. They're part of your parents' secret world and it sometimes takes a while before they talk about them with anyone else. Only they know why they chose to share their lives. The things that brought them together in the first place and then kept them together over time aren't always clear-cut and obvious to everyone else. In some couples' cases their parents may have put pressure on them to get married because they felt it was inappropriate for two people to have a sexual relationship without being husband and wife. For others, the fear of being alone may have led to marriage without their really getting to know each other well enough in the first place.

If your parents are not as close as they used to be, it's possible that

understand

one or both of them may start another relationship with someone else—
or have already. Just like children, adults develop and change over the
course of their lives and it's possible for them to fall in love for a second
time. Your parents' new relationships may be quite different from the
one they had together, but they can be just as important and strong and
beautiful. But obviously, for these new relationships to continue, the
current one between them must end.

Mary can remember how her mother suddenly became really forget-
ful and seemed to spend her day in a dream world. She would be all
smiles one moment and in tears the next. Mary knew that something was
wrong but just could not put her finger on why her mother's moods had
become so unpredictable. She was in the dark right up till the moment

when her mother finally packed her bags. It was really hard to come to grips with, but at least Mary finally understood what was going on. Today, she's happy again, and so is her mother. And while her father was probably really hurt by her mother's new relationship at first, he seems better now, and mentions someone named Susan more and more each time Mary sees him.

In some cases, the reasons for the breakup are more visible because they're more dramatic—for example, if one parent just can't take any more of the other's alcoholism, drug use, or violence. Unfortunately, newspapers are full of tragic stories of mothers or fathers abusing their children, or each other. If this is happening to you, you need to get help immediately. Physical violence is against the law, and you don't have to put up with it, whether it's happening to you or another family member. There are people who can help you stop the abuse, and to deal with the

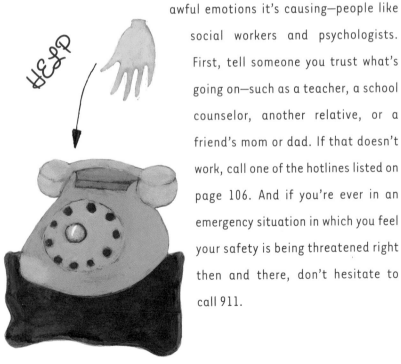

awful emotions it's causing—people like social workers and psychologists. First, tell someone you trust what's going on—such as a teacher, a school counselor, another relative, or a friend's mom or dad. If that doesn't work, call one of the hotlines listed on page 106. And if you're ever in an emergency situation in which you feel your safety is being threatened right then and there, don't hesitate to call 911.

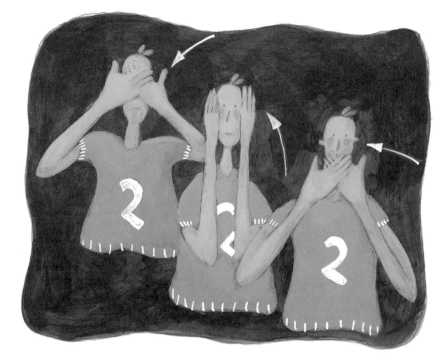

what's happening
to me?

Everyone reacts in his or her own way when faced with difficult situations like divorce, because everyone's personality and way of dealing is different. You might make like an ostrich and bury your head in the sand so you don't have to see or hear what's going on around you. Hiding away seems like a pretty good idea when it seems as if anything you do might cause another major scene. On the other hand, you may feel like telling the world what's happening, from your best friend, to his little brother, to the guy who works at the grocery store checkout; it just makes you feel better to be able to vent about your problems.

ph1

21

Other people want to fight back. They shout and scream, threaten to run away, beg their parents to stay together, promise not to watch television before they've finished their homework — anything to feel as if they have some effect on the situation. In addition to any of these reactions, you might also feel lost, abandoned, caught in the middle of the conflict, or so angry about it that you hate everyone, including your mother and father. You might get moody, argue with your friends, or neglect your homework or after-school activities. Or you might do the opposite—studying or playing even harder to try and lose yourself in your efforts.

There's nothing abnormal about any of these ways of coping. They're all methods of expressing your confusion and emotional distress—although some of them (for example, talking) are healthier than others (such as cutting class).

Don't forget that, whatever happens, your parents will always be the people who love you and care about you. The joy you bring your parents isn't going to fade or disappear, even if it seems harder to see at times, when they're busy being so angry at each other. Your parents will remain the two people who brought you into the world. They love you and you love them—even if you feel like yelling and screaming at them much of the time. Go ahead! It might remind them that you're still there, full of questions and worries. It might remind them of the deal they struck with you when you were born—that the world no longer revolves around them alone, and that caring for you is more important than anything else.

what part do i play
in all this?

Say one particularly miserable evening you hear your parents arguing about who made the mess in the living room or who's going to pick you up from soccer practice. Now your mind is probably racing: What if I hadn't been born—would they still be madly in love? Are they upset with each other because I was in an obnoxious mood the other night? Or is it because I fight with my older sister? Does that change the way they feel about each other? Does it affect the patience they have for each other?

We're here to tell you once and for all that you don't need to worry about any of that. What's going on between them has nothing to do with you or your existence. Just because they aren't getting along with each other, that doesn't change anything about the way they feel about you.

Their fighting has nothing to do with your behavior either. Even if you were the perfect teenager, it wouldn't change the situation. You might feel guilty because you can't see what's really causing their disagreements, and so you mistakenly feel that you're responsible. Being left in the dark, on the outside of all the turmoil, you might feel the need to find a reason for their fighting and their breakup, and the only thing you can come up with is that you're a burden to them. But remember: you can't control your parents. They're responsible for their own actions, and you are in no way to blame.

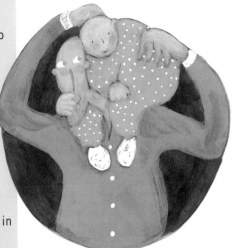

Still, knowing that isn't going to stop you from feeling overwhelmed by conflicting emotions—feelings not only of love and hate, but also of reproach, pity, and exasperation toward one or both of your parents. For example, maybe you think your mother is to blame for all the arguments; she's impossible to live with, she's always complaining, she works too hard or doesn't go out enough, or doesn't have a life of her own. You might feel she doesn't try hard enough to be flexible or understanding—but then you find yourself wanting to defend her when your father criticizes her.

And then you start to think maybe your father is entirely to blame. He yells for no reason and leaves without any warning. You hate him because of the violent conflict he causes. But you also remember all the times he's been so loving toward you, when you did things together and he was as gentle as a lamb. How can your dad have two such different sides to his character? How can your mom not realize she's driving him away? It's no wonder you resent them for not being more open about what's going on and for making you feel so confused.

growing up is
hard to do

It's hard to accept the idea that your parents don't love each other anymore. It probably seems like just yesterday that you were one close, connected unit. They were the two solid rocks that you relied on—you could ask them anything you wanted—their life pretty much belonged to you. You admired them and needed them, and you wanted to grow up to be just like them.

Facing their separation won't be easy; you'll have to learn to let go of the single relationship you had with your parents—the one in which Mom and Dad were sort of like a single person who loved you. From now on, you'll have to build a pair of relationships—one with your dad and one with your mom.

Being on the brink or in the midst of adolescence while all this is happening doesn't make it any easier. Both your body and your mind are undergoing such major changes that it'd be nice to have the stability of your parents' relationship to rely on as you assert your independence, challenging their views on life and forming your own opinions about things. But now that they're about to split up, you might feel more like taking a step backward than moving ahead. Still, it doesn't have to happen like that. You'll have to try even harder to make sure their problems as a couple don't become your problems. You'll need to learn how to distinguish between their conflicts and the conflicts that teenagers naturally face with their parents as they're growing up.

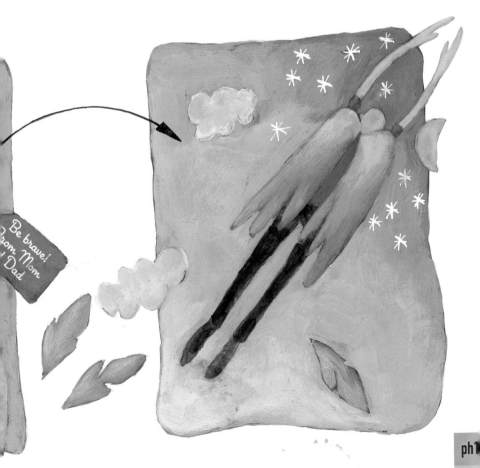

my childhood

Even if parents sometimes seem to belong to a completely different species, it helps if you can get your head around the fact that they're ordinary people, just like everyone else. And just like everyone else, they're allowed to break down sometimes, to feel lost, and in need of support.

It might seem ridiculous when they argue about who gets to keep the iron or the Beatles collection—you didn't think they could ever be so petty or fight so fiercely over such unimportant things. But sometimes, fighting about the small stuff actually masks much bigger issues. The objects themselves suddenly become incredibly significant—and sometimes things get blown way out of proportion. One parent might say: "My mother gave us that iron when Charlotte was born." The other might feel so attached to the CDs, because of the memories they hold, that they can't bear to part with them.

heroes

While this kind of stuff is going on, your mom or dad may well turn to you in an attempt to get you on their side, to find an ally to help them justify their decision to leave. They might say things like: "Didn't you hear your father say exactly the opposite last night?" or "Listen to how your mother talks to me!" Or speaking to each other, they might say, "You're never around anymore—even your son/daughter has noticed!" But dragging you into the middle and making you choose sides isn't fair to you, and they shouldn't do it. They're the adults and it's their responsibility to be mature and keep you out of their arguments. If they're having a momentary lapse and seem to have forgotten that, it's important for you to try to be stronger than they are. Don't let yourself get sucked in. Say, "You two need to work this out on your own. I don't want to be involved." Just listening to their fighting is hard enough; you shouldn't have to referee.

playing judge

Still, you might be feeling the urge to play judge in all of this and defend the parent you consider to be "the victim." But it's really not up to you to take on this role. Just think of how much you hate it when your parents intervene in disputes between you and your brothers or sisters—it's not their fight so they should stay out of it, right? Besides, conflicts are rarely clear-cut, with an evil villain on one side and an innocent victim on the other. Things are more complicated than that, and the reasons your mom and dad are fighting may relate to events that you didn't experienced firsthand, things that are part of their history alone.

Whatever the subject matter of the fight, you may find yourself automatically springing to the defense of the parent you feel closest to, or the one you feel you have the most in common with. It all depends on your individual situation and the relationship you've developed with your parents over the course of your life. You might not even know why you tend to pull for one side or the other—a lot of it has to do with psychological reactions coming from deep inside.

Some adults feel so upset and helpless at the failure of their marriage that they resort to reassuring themselves by fishing for affection from their children. They'll indulge themselves by asking things like "Who do you like best—Mom or Dad?" and "Who do you think is right and wrong in all of this, me or your father?" It's important to protect yourself by remaining neutral. If you kiss your mom, make sure you kiss your dad, too. They are both your parents and even if you love them differently, you don't have to prove how deeply you feel about either of them. Tell them that you love them both and that it's impossible for you to choose between them.

Mom   Dad

good-bye to childhood

Your childhood is coming to an end and with it goes the illusion that nothing bad is ever going to happen to you. And that's a tough thing to face.

You're in the process of letting go of childish things, of saying good-bye to the little girl or boy inside you. The big, wide world is beckoning you and you're getting more and more curious about what it has in store, and what it's like to grow up and experience all the great things that being an adult has to offer. You feel grown up enough to be independent from your parents, even though you know that this isn't going to happen just yet.

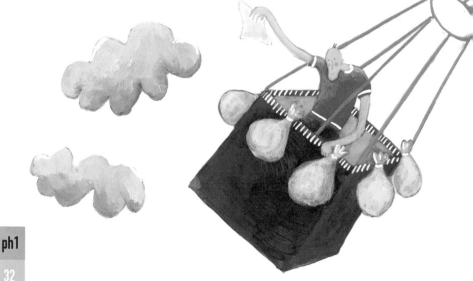

You feel confident about being able to choose what books you want to read, what movies to see, and which friends to hang out with, without needing to ask your parents' advice. Your attitude toward adults is probably changing, too. As time goes by, your parents will slowly transform from untouchable, idealized, totally perfect figures into people who have good and bad qualities, just like everyone else. And with that realization often comes the urge to criticize their way of life. It becomes harder and harder to respect their wishes and obey them when you feel as if you know what's best for yourself. Your parents' separation may force you to grow up even faster. You'll learn to adapt to new situations, some that are difficult to handle. And since you'll have a separate relationship with each parent, you may become more independent from both of them—although that doesn't mean you'll have any less of a close and loving relationship with either one.

call:
Pat   Louis
Donna
     Tonya

my accomplices

DIVORCE and

do I agree or disagree?

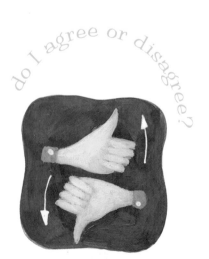

A LEGAL ACT

the divorce

When a situation becomes really unbearable, divorce can be the lesser of two evils, according to Françoise Dolt, the famous French psychoanalyst. The aim of this legal act is to fix a situation that has become difficult for both parents and children, and the goal is to bring about the best solution for everyone involved. The act is made legal by a family court judge who is subject to the laws governing the state and the country.

The most important thing the judge does is to defend the interests of the children of the two people divorcing and to ensure that their rights are respected. These rights include the right to education, to be cared for, to be kept safe, to live in a decent home, and to be loved. All these factors are considered by the judge when he or she makes decisions about what will happen after the divorce.

When two people divorce, the judge, in his or her role as a representative of the law, officially recognizes the end of the marriage and works with the couple and their lawyers to make all the necessary arrangements, such as who gets what property (the house, the car, etc.) and which parent the kids will live with.

The act of divorcing frees your parents from their responsibilities and duties to each other—but never the responsibility they have to you and your brothers and sisters. Today, there are several types of divorce, and the legal terms and subtle meanings involved can be pretty complicated. We'll try to explain the major differences here.

no fault

A no-fault divorce means that neither the husband nor the wife places blame for the failure of the marriage on the other—in other words, no one is at fault, at least as far the courts are concerned. A no-fault divorce can come about in one of two ways. One way is that both the husband and wife agree to divorce—they both want to separate. The other way is that only one of them wants to divorce. The person who wants a divorce can get one even if the other person doesn't want it, as

long as certain requirements are met. These requirements vary from state to state, but they usually involve things like the couple being emotionally or physically separated for a certain set period of time, and/or having "irreconcilable differences," which is a fancy way of saying they don't get along anymore.

If your parents are getting a no-fault divorce, their next step is to decide things like where you and your brothers and sisters should live, how much child support must be paid, and how to divide their joint possessions. Each parent is usually represented by a lawyer, and the lawyers help them negotiate and come to an agreement on all these different things—this is called a separation agreement. If your parents do reach an agreement, then

they go to a family-court judge. The judge verifies that the agreement is fair to both your mom and your dad and is in your best interest, and then ratifies their decision. The whole process for this type of divorce can take anywhere from about a month and a half to a year— it usually becomes final in a matter of days or weeks after the couple reaches an agreement.

If your parents can't reach an agreement, however, a trial will be held at which their lawyers present evidence to the judge, and then the judge makes all the major decisions on child custody, child support, and who gets what property, such as the house and the car. In this case, the divorce can take longer—sometimes up to two years.

fault

A fault divorce is more complicated and takes longer. In this type of divorce, the husband and wife try to place blame on each other and to demonstrate that certain marital obligations were not fulfilled by the other, causing the need for the marriage to end.

Reasons for a spouse to be blamed for the need for a divorce include violence, alcoholism, adultery (when one person has a relationship with someone outside the marriage), abandonment of the family home, etc.

While these things are usually attributed to one parent, there are also cases of shared blame, meaning that blame has been attributed to each parent. During this type of divorce, your parents have to demonstrate and prove to a judge all the wrongs inflicted upon them by their spouse. In some states, the decision about which person is to blame affects the decision about how much of the joint property they get to keep, and things like that; in other states, it doesn't make a difference at all. Except in cases where both parents are in agreement, it is the judge who makes the decisions about where the child or children should live, about visiting rights, and about child support, just like in a no-fault divorce in which the parents can't reach an agreement. But the best interests of the child are always considered to be the most important thing when the judge makes these decisions.

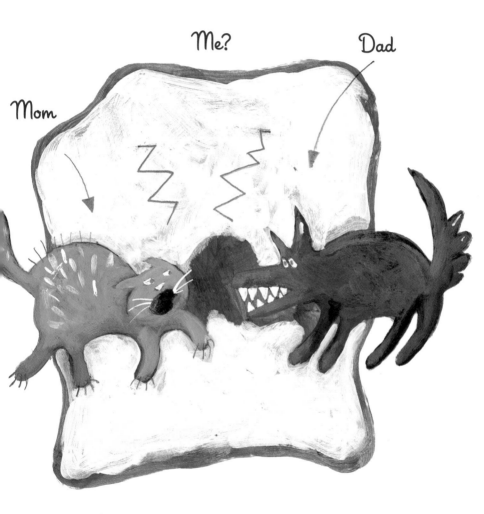

don't i get

Your parents and the family-court judge make all the
decisions about where and with which parent you'll live after the
divorce. Your mom or dad may ask you what you want to do, or they may
decide for you. But in almost all cases in which your parents disagree
about whom you should live with, you will be asked your opinion. A
lawyer may be appointed to represent you, and the judge may ask you to
come into his office, along with a court reporter and your mom's and
dad's lawyers. (Your mom and dad themselves, however, will not be in
the room—and they're generally not supposed to be told anything you
say to the judge.) The judge will ask you questions about your life at
home, to get a feel for what's best for you. There's no pressure, no right
or wrong answers. And you don't have to worry about choosing sides
between your parents—it's not your responsibility to decide between

Social
worker

Lawyer

say?

them, and the judge will likely not even ask straight out whom you want to live with. However, you're free to volunteer that information yourself if you want to. Again, it's the judge's job to act not according to your wishes, but according to your best interests, so he may not always pick the same parent that you say you want to live with. However, the older you are, the more weight the judge will place on your opinion.

This aspect of the proceedings may seem difficult or frightening. But take it from one boy named Adrian: once he understood that the judge was there to protect his parents, brother, and sisters from the painful repercussions of the separation, he felt immensely relieved. "I thought that going to court meant you could go to prison. But the judge explained everything and really reassured me. Until then, I was really afraid for my parents."

Judge

what happens if my parents can't agree?

The family-court judge will resolve the dispute and make the final decision. Your parents will have to respect the decision, which will always be made with your best interests in mind. The judge will consider both parents' arguments and your feelings, and may also consult experts such as psychologists or social workers to get their opinions on what's best for you.

what happens
now?

If your parents have agreed on joint custody, they'll both continue to make most major decisions about your upbringing together, even though you live with one of them part of the time and the other the rest of the time. On the other hand, if your mom or dad has sole custody, he or she alone has the right to make these decisions—things like what religion you should be raised in, or whether you'll go to public or private school. However, it's almost always a part of the separation agreement that the custodial parent must consult with the other parent to get his or her opinion on these matters. And if that parent really dis-

Parent

agrees with something, he or she can take the issue to court and have a judge rule as to whether the decision is in your best interest.

You will live with the parent granted custody. In the past, most children lived with their mother after a divorce. It was something that just seemed natural: since the beginning of time, in both humans and animals, the mother has been the one to nourish and care for her young, feeding, cradling, protecting, and educating them. The father is more often the one who provides food and shelter for the family, and maybe later on, acts as a social educator to the child. Until recently in our society, women usually worked in the home and could therefore spend more time with their children than men could. However, society is changing and more and more fathers now find it unfair that children

Sunday, August 15th
Mom

Monday, August 16th
Dad

should automatically live with their mothers. They feel they can look after their children just as well as the mothers can. Some men have proved this to be true in court and been awarded custody. For example, if a father has a job that allows him greater flexibility than his ex-wife and wants custody of his child, then a judge may very well grant it.

In deciding whether you should live with your mother or father, the judge will always avoid separating you from your brothers and sisters unless absolutely necessary, or unless you and your parents specially request this for some reason. But in the vast majority of cases, you will all stay together

The parent you don't live with—known as the "noncustodial parent"—will usually have visiting rights; that means you'll probably have a schedule of days when you'll stay at his or her house. Often, that's every other weekend. Which holidays you'll spend with which parent may also be pre-arranged. For example, it may be decided that you'll spend holidays during the first half of the year with one parent and holidays during the second half of the year with the other parent, and then vice versa the next

year. On the other hand, your parents may decide to keep this schedule looser, and figure it out as you all go along. If your parents live in different towns, you might make fewer visits, but stay longer for each one.

If you're dividing your time between your mom's house and your dad's house, the judge will try to ensure that you don't have to change schools and continually uproot yourself. This would be a concern if your parents agreed that you should spend one week with one parent and then the following week with the other. For this to be allowed, your parents would need to live reasonably close to each other so that you'd be in the same school district at both houses. Your parents would also need to be on good terms with each other for the arrangement to work well.

Since you're getting older now, you should speak up and let your parents know if you have strong feelings about how the visitation schedule should work. Although, just as with everything else, your parents and the judge are the ones who will ultimately decide what happens.

are decisions made in a divorce judgment final?

Yes and no. The arrangements made in court are expected to be followed for the foreseeable future. But one or both of your parents can petition the court to amend part of the decision if they have good reason, for example, if the parent you live with plans to move far away, or one of them loses his or her job. In these cases, the judge can make a revised ruling, again focussing on the best interests of the child.

This happened to one boy named Charles. His parents divorced when he was ten years old. He recalls how his mother wanted a complete change of environment so that she could make a new start after the divorce. She found an apartment far away from the one she and Charles's father had lived in before the divorce, which meant that Charles would have to leave his school and his friends in the middle of the school year. With the agreement of both of Charles's parents, the judge ruled that he should stay with his father in the family home until the end of the school year. "That made it much easier for me," says Charles. "I didn't have to drop everything suddenly and instead could gradually get used to my new life. I didn't tell my friends that I was moving till later on. It would have been too hard to explain about the divorce and moving all at the same time."

getting used
to things

As Charles makes clear, adapting to a new life takes time. It's not always easy to get used to the changes, especially if you're going through a dramatic one, such as a move to a new town. It helps to try to keep to a regular schedule. For example, if you were on the soccer team at your old school, join the team at your new school. Or if you've always done your homework on Sunday afternoons, keep doing it that way, even if you now spend Sundays at your other parents' house.

While you try to keep some things about your new life the same,

other things will inevitably be different. But different doesn't always mean bad. In fact, spending time separately with each of your parents might make you closer to both of them. And it might even give you the opportunity to try out new things. Say your family has always lived in the city because that's where your mom's job is, but now your dad is moving out to the country. Now when you stay with him, you'll be able to do all kinds of stuff you rarely got to before, such as hiking in the woods, camping, swimming, and skiing. Or maybe now that you'll have more one-on-one time with your mom, the two of you can check out that museum you've been meaning to visit—or maybe rent that sappy romance on DVD that your father would never have gone for! Learning to adapt to different lifestyles can really help broaden your mind. What's good for your father may not necessarily be good for your mother, so you'll likely end up doing things differently with each of them, and neither way will be any better or worse than the other—just different. It's up to you to learn along with your parents, and to come to terms with your new way of life. Once the structure of your new lifestyle is settled and flowing smoothly, you might be able to change certain things, after talking it through with your parents. If all three of you can come to an agreement, then there's nothing stopping you from making little adjustments to the general framework determined by the court.

what if my parents
aren't
married?

Your parents may not have formalized their relationship with a marriage certificate. More and more couples live together today as partners rather than as husband and wife. Society has changed and it's more accepted now for parents not to be married. But this doesn't mean that they don't have the same responsibilities toward you. Protecting the best interests of children whose parents aren't married is just as important as protecting them for children whose parents are married.

When your parents split up, they'll have to make the same decisions and arrangements that they would if they were legally married. First and foremost, they'll have to decide whom you'll live with. And just as with married parents, the one you don't end up living with will have to pay child support to help the other parent care for you. And they'll have to decide when and how often you'll visit your other parent. The big difference between married parents and unmarried parents is that married parents have to get their decisions finalized by a judge, even if they fully agree on everything. If unmarried parents agree on everything, they can just go ahead with their decisions, without going to court and seeing a judge. But, even though they don't have to, it's a good idea for them to go to a judge and have their agreement made official anyway. That way the court can make sure their arrangements are fair to both of them, and that both of them abide by the decisions they've made now and in the future, since they'll be legally bound to do so.

what happens if they disagree?

If your parents come to an agreement, the judge will not intervene in their separation. However, if they argue about whom you should live with, they can hire lawyers and ask a judge to decide for them. Just as with custody cases of married parents, the judge will most likely take you aside to talk, to help him get a feel for what's in your best interest.

child support

One of the consequences of divorce is that the noncustodial
parent must contribute financially to the education and care of the
child. He or she must pay child support to the other parent. The amount
of money to be paid is determined by the income of each parent and the
needs of the child. Both of these factors may change as you get older,
and so one of your parents may petition the court to change the child-

support amount at some point in the future. Some kids feel guilty about all this, particularly if they know that the parent paying child support doesn't have a lot of money to spare. You might feel like a burden to him or her. But that is not the case at all. Child support is a legal obligation imposed by the court. If your parents had stayed together, both of them would be contributing to your care, so now that they're separated, child support is put in place to make sure both parents keep contributing. Besides, even though they're divorcing each other, your parents love you just the same and want to make sure you have everything you need.

what happens if the child support isn't paid?

If the parent you don't live with isn't paying the child support that he or she is required to according to the divorce decree (that is, the set of decisions approved by the judge), there are things your other parent can do to collect it. Every state has a child support enforcement agency. This agency can help track down the parent who's not paying, sue him or her for the money owed, or deduct the money directly out of his or her pay check. But this isn't something for you to worry about, and it won't affect whether or not you're allowed to see your parent. Noncustodial parents can't be prevented from visiting their kids just because they're not paying the child support they're supposed to.

who can i count on?

Through all of this, you're bound to feel sad, upset, or even betrayed, and you might be wondering whom you can rely on now that your family's broken up. The answer is that you can still count on both your parents—just separately. While it would be great if you felt comfortable confiding in both of them, it's okay if you find yourself opening up to one more than the other. Maybe your mom seems to understand your feelings more and be more sympathetic. Or maybe you feel closer to your father now that he's no longer arguing with your mother. Either way, you'll probably start to see your parents in a new light and your relationships with them will become more mature.

Still, not all the tension will end the day one of your parents moves out. One or both of them may have a hard time adjusting to their new life, just as you might. Discovering their freedom again could make them feel lost and disoriented, and become difficult to live with. They may still be suffering from the shock of the separation and have less patience than before. Little faults that were part of the jigsaw puzzle of everyday family life become much more pronounced. When faced with their failure as a couple, some parents feel really angry and behave in unusual ways. It might even seem like they've lost interest in you. That, or they take things out on you by handing out punishments left and right.

In this situation, the parent you feel most comfortable with, maybe your mom, can help you to resolve these conflicts. You can also try to explain calmly to the parent you're having trouble with, maybe your dad, that you are not responsible for what he is going through and that he needs to work these problems out on his own so you can get your relationship with him back to what it should be. With luck, this will be a wake-up call to your parents and will help them focus on their real priority (you!). If it doesn't work and your time at home continues to mean one headache and stomachache after another, there are some other people you can turn to for support.

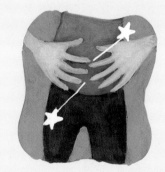

your friends

Talking to friends—especially ones whose parents are divorced—can really help. They'll let you vent, and will understand what you're feeling since they've been there, done that. It feels good to know that you're not the only one who's had to deal with such a difficult situation, and confiding in others who have can really make you feel less isolated. That's not to say that close friends whose parents are still together can't provide the same support. But if you know of someone who can relate to what's going on in your family, you can ask them the questions you're grappling with right now, such as "Do you ever wish they'd stayed together? What was it like visiting your mom/dad at the new house? I'm feeling kind of angry at them right now—did you feel that way, too? Does it last?" They'll tell you what happened to them and you'll share your own experiences. They'll lend a sympathetic and understanding ear, and so will you. Even if this doesn't solve all your problems, it'll still help you feel like someone cares about what's going on with you, which makes anything easier to deal with.

Virginia turned to one of her girlfriends when her parents divorced. "I was lost. If Sophie hadn't been there for me, I would have run away. My parents argued and fought all the time. One day my mother woke up with a black eye and told me she had banged it on the door. But I knew that she was lying to me because I had heard them shouting. They would explode with anger, and I was even afraid they might hurt me sometimes. It seemed like nothing could stop them from fighting. Sophie's mom suggested I come to stay with her family for a while. I really feel safe at her house."

your grandpar

Grandparents are your roots in life. Whether or not you're super-close to them right now, the fact that you're family connects you in a deep and lasting way. And because your relationship with your grandparents isn't in the midst of an upheaval, the way your relationship with your parents is, they might be able to be there for you while you work through this.

Of course, everyone's grandparents are different, but many are especially good at spoiling their grandkids. Things like homemade chocolate cake that reminds you of when you were young and everything was perfect, or some money slipped into your pocket before you leave can do wonders for your mood. These little gestures show you that they love you and are there for you.

On the other hand, some grandparents will openly take sides with their son or daughter during a divorce. It's sort of understandable—no parent likes to see his or her child suffer. So before you go hitting them up for candy, cash, or a shoulder to cry on, it's important to give your grandparents some time to process what's happening. If they're not yet being the loving, mature, supportive relatives they should be, try not to be overly sensitive to things they say or do. All of this is often just a reflection of how much they, too, are upset by the divorce. In the long run, none of this will jeopardize your relationship with them.

nts

your other
relatives

Maybe you've got an Aunt Christine and Uncle Peter who've been married for something like twenty-five years, and have three or four children. They're solid and reliable and you'd love to be adopted into their clan, just for a little while, just to feel like part of a whole family again. If you've got relatives like these, your parents' divorce could be a real opportunity to reconnect with them, and to make friends with your cousins (and maybe discover they're not the spoiled brats or nerds you thought they were). Your extended family may be a good place to turn for sympathy and support. They're adults who live outside the storm raging at home, so you can rely on them for a little stability and comfort.

Unless of course your Aunt Christine and Uncle Peter are raging right along with your parents. Unfortunately, in some families a separation can mean an opportunity for some serious score-settling. The parent who leaves becomes the target of criticism and the family uses him or her as someone to offload all their pent-up bitterness on. People who vent their feelings about one parent think they're protecting the other parent—the "victim" in the situation. But while it might give them some satisfaction, it's not helping you out any. After all, that's your mom or dad they're hurling insults at! It probably seems like just yesterday that all your relatives were curled up around a fire together during the holi-

days. Now half of them are treating your dad like public enemy number one, and your mom is acting a little like an overindulgent child basking in all the attention, and not sticking up for your father at all. Or vice versa. If that sounds about right, you might be asking yourself at this point, "What if they're right and my mom/dad really is to blame?" Even if they don't know what they're talking about, these kinds of inconsiderate relatives can sow the seeds of doubt in your mind and put you back at square one, coming up with reasons for your parents' split that really don't have any basis in fact.

The thing to do is stick your fingers in your ears and not listen to any of the nasty things that are said. They have nothing to do with you. Time will make everyone calm down and their resentment will fade when your parents manage to bring some balance back into their lives again. Try to maintain relationships with family members on both sides—your mom's and your dad's. If, for example, your mother wants to cut all ties with her mother-in-law, it's up to her to make this decision for herself; it doesn't mean you have to do the same. If she asks you to, don't feel obliged to say yes. From now on, you need to be able to stand up to your parents and say no if they ask you to do things like this that don't seem right.

a new nest

In the coming months, you're going to have to get used to a differ-ent way of life, a new environment at home. The most likely possibility is that you'll stay in the same house, but you'll have to come to terms with the fact that one of your parents doesn't live there anymore. A photo-graph, a lingering scent in a closet, an item of clothing left behind — all these little things can stir memories and emotions. Don't feel as though you have to bury these emotions. The fact is that you're missing someone and finding it hard to cope with his or her absence, which is totally normal. It might help to hang up a picture of your mom or dad, or even to put something of hers or his on your desk so at least it feels like your missing parent is there in spirit.

If you have to move to a new home or spend every other weekend at a new house, there'll be fewer familiar places and things to remind you of your past. Making a new "nest" and filling it with new memories takes time. Bring a few things you love to the new house. Decorate your new room with posters or photos to make it more homey. And even if you're just staying there several times a month, see if you can invite friends to come over and hang out some time soon—it'll help you put down new roots and really make the place feel like your place, rather than a hotel where you crash every now and then.

Getting settled in won't be super-easy, especially if you're moving away permanently to a new town. You'll have to start again from scratch with a new home, new friends, and a new school. But who's to say all of these new things won't be as good—or even better—than the old ones? Be brave and make the effort to meet new people as soon as you get there. Joining after-school clubs or getting involved in team sports are two great, easy, low-stress ways to start building a new social circle.

living in
two houses

When the weekend comes and it's time to go visit the parent you don't live with, you may have some mixed feelings about the whole thing. You probably feel happy and sad at the same time—excited about seeing your mom or dad, but also anxious or guilty about the parent you're leaving behind at home. You might also feel a little annoyed that you have to drop everything, pack a bag, and leave what you consider "home" to go to another home for two days, or however long your visit is. Then, at the end of the weekend, you might feel sad again because you know you won't see your mom or dad for two weeks. And you might now feel bad about now leaving *this* parent all alone. Obviously they're your parents, you love them, and you want to protect them. But you also need to realize that leaving them will not do them any major harm. It was their choice to separate, and they need to deal with the changes that come along with that choice.

They may sometimes drop questions into the conversation, like: "What did you do this weekend? Did you like it at Mom's place? What time did you go to bed?" They have every right to be curious because you've been away from them for a while, just as they want to know what you did when you've been away at a friend's house overnight. The difference here is that there may be some ulterior motives driving your parents' questions. Your mom might want to know more details so that she can reassure herself that you're okay when she's not there. Or, your dad might subconsciously be hoping to find that something went wrong, so he can reassure himself that things go better when he's around. Both your mom and your dad want to feel that they're needed, that they're important to your daily life and your happiness. In time, they'll realize that just because you have a blast with one of them doesn't mean you don't need the other one. Until then, they may give you the third degree about what happens when you go away. It's okay to be honest and tell them all about it, but it's also okay if you're not always in the mood. It could be that it's a part of your life you're not yet ready to share with the parent who wasn't there to experience it.

It's just like your not always wanting to tell every detail of your life to your friends, or to share information about what you do with one friend with another friend. Some kids would rather keep this very personal part of their life between themselves and either their mom or their dad—not because they have anything to hide, but because it is their life and they feel more comfortable keeping the two different parts of it private.

On the other hand, if you don't mind sharing details with your other parent, you should still be careful about what

you say and how you say it. Don't be immature and manipulative by saying things like: "I'm allowed to stay up an hour later at Dad's place!" or
"Mom doesn't force me to make my bed!" You might think it's a good
strategy for getting what you want, but it will only make your parent
angry, or even prompt him or her to criticize the ways things are done at
your other parent's house, neither of which you want to happen.

i am not a
mailman!

In your parents' minds, you're sort of the one remaining link
between them. And that may tempt them to treat
you as an intermediary. If whatever it was they
used to fight about still isn't really resolved,
the arguments could continue on, through
you. Nicholas remembers having to deliver
letters between his parents. He hated
being their personal mailman and would just
leave the letters on the table or the desk, hoping
the parent it was meant for would find it. But when he
or she did, Nicholas would have to listen to what the letters said. One day it all became too much for him and he wrote

letters of his own to each parent explaining that he would no longer play the go-between, and that the miraculous new technology known as the telephone was the best way of communicating—even for divorced parents. His mom and dad got the message and apologized for behaving badly. Using Nicholas as a message bearer was a way for his parents to avoid confrontation; but it's not up to kids to play this role. Whatever your parents want to say to each other is their business and should be kept between them. Explain to them that delivering their messages—whether verbal, written, or otherwise—makes you uncomfortable, then reassure them that you love them both equally and that their problems as a couple will never change that.

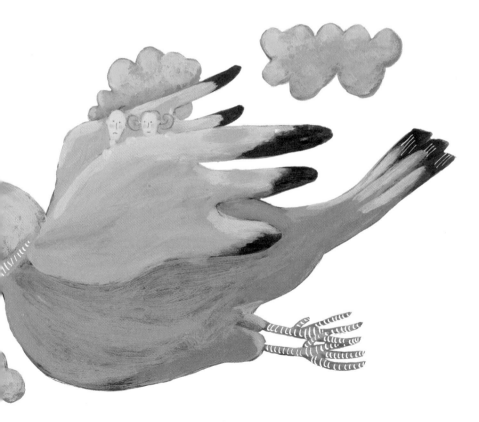

i'm not my mom and i'm not my dad,
i'm just me!

Just because your mom and dad have split up, it doesn't mean that the arguments will come to a complete and immediate halt, as you're probably finding out. Many of their issues may have been resolved, but some bitterness and regret could linger. Feelings of pain over the separation are still there, whether spoken or unspoken, because it takes more than a legal judgement or separate houses to make this pain go away. Imagine if you broke up with a girlfriend or boyfriend—simply not seeing the person wouldn't cure your broken heart overnight. Wounds need time to heal.

But you shouldn't have to be caught in the crossfire of your parents' continued disagreements. If you have to endure comments like: "Your mother could have bought you a pair of sneakers" or "That's just like your father. He never understood anything about kids," tell them you don't want to hear it. Say "I am not my mom or dad—I'm just me." If they don't get that you want to be left out of their conflicts and don't enjoy hearing them criticize each other, you might try suggesting—delicately— that they consider seeing a psychologist or family therapist, someone outside the family circle who can offer unbiased advice. He or she can listen to them (so you don't have to!) and try to help them resolve issues linked to the separation, and figure out ways to avoid involving you in their problems.

pain and hurt

Alison once had a stomachache for over a week. Her mother took her to the doctor, but he couldn't find anything wrong with her. Simon isn't sleeping well at night. At four in the morning he sits in the kitchen, nibbling on chocolate. "All these thoughts are going around in my head. I'm afraid that if I go to sleep something bad might happen."

Feeling sick or just "not well" is a normal reaction to the emotional pain and anxiety you go through during a divorce. It's so hard to express in words all the confusing and sometimes contradictory feelings that you're experiencing. So your mind instead sends an alarm signal to the body in the form of a stomachache or headache to warn you that things aren't right.

Of course you should feel free to pop an aspirin or some Pepto to make yourself feel better. But remember that medication can't heal the deep-down reasons for your pain. The support of your family and friends is much more likely to help cure the anxiety that's behind all your physical symptoms.

Again, you can turn to your friends or other trusted members of your family for help; just know that they're not always in a position to listen without taking sides. If that turns out to be the case for you, talking to a neutral third party could be your best bet. A school counselor should be able to refer you to a psychologist, possibly at little or no cost, who will listen to what you have to say, answer your questions, and/or try to find a solution to your problems. He or she will not judge you or your parents. With no loyalties or commitments to anyone in your family, he or she will able to give you a completely unbiased opinion.

After her parents divorced, Julie went to see a psychologist. "At last I could tell someone what was on my mind without feeling like I was causing anyone pain or being a pain. Everything came out—all my anger, hurt, and tears. After each session, I was exhausted but relieved. I feel so much better now, and I look at my parents a little differently. What they're going through has nothing to do with me. But I know that I love them and they love me."

more children

THE START OF

EACH PERSON
PLAYS A PART

A BIG CHANGE

no great shakes

what's your name?

A NEW LIFE

family HISTORIES

a moment of

Unless your parents left each other for new partners, they'll have to spend some time living on their own, licking their wounds, and regaining self-confidence. Getting serious with someone new is probably not high on their list of priorities at this stage. Before starting a new family they need to spend time rebuilding their own emotional strength and learning to understand and love themselves, so that others can love them, too. Your mom and dad need to accept that they've lost a partner and to grieve for the relationship they thought would last forever.

This period is important for you, too—it's your time to recover and to learn how to be flexible and open to change. You'll need to adapt your relationship with each of your parents to the new situation. It'll help a lot if you spend time with each of them, maybe going shopping, cooking dinner, or just talking with them quietly, alone. Things will be different from before. Each of your parents will find his or her way of handling life, moving forward or developing a part of his or her personality that may have been hidden or held back during the inevitable compromises made during marriage. This could turn out to be a really great opportunity for you, so make the most of the situation. Now's the time to get out anything that's been weighing on your mind, to clear up

alm

any misunderstandings between you and your parents, and to negotiate any parts of your situation that you're not happy about, whether they seem related to the divorce or not. You'll learn to make up your own mind about issues independent of what your parents believe (not that you'll always get your way). And you'll learn how to live under the care of one parent at a time, instead of both together.

You may also get some new and different responsibilities. Maybe you'll have to pick up your little sister after school, do the grocery shopping, or help clean the house. Since there's only one parent to handle all the chores now, it'll really help out if you can take some of them on. It'll also prove what a mature and responsible kid you are, which could help *you* out when it comes to deciding on curfews, allowance, and things like that.

Speaking of money, any financial problems your family might have had over the years probably went over your head, for the most part. There were most likely two salaries coming in, or maybe the parent that has now moved out was the one who supported the whole family. Either way, how your family—and therefore you—deals with money will probably change somewhat now that you're living with just one parent.

tightening your belt

When parents divorce, it leaves just one income per household. For a lot of families, this means they'll need to tighten the budget, despite the additional money coming in from child support.

As a teenager, it can be especially difficult to accept this kind of change. Just as you're starting to go to the movies every week with your friends, suddenly you have to cut back to just once a month. You're dying for all the great clothes you've seen on kids at school—the kind your parents used to buy you all the time—but now you're only allowed to go shopping once for fall and once for spring.

No one can blame you for feeling angry or bitter toward your parents because it was their decision that turned your life upside down. And you wouldn't be the first to resort to pleading with one parent to buy you all the stuff that the other one says you can't afford. And if that one parent is doing fairly well financially, he or she might say yes. But don't go behind your other parent's back in a manipulative way—in all likelihood, they'll both figure out what's going on and you might get in trouble. After all, it's not only about the money, but also about how your parents want to raise you—about which things they believe you should be allowed to spend money on, and which you shouldn't. So it's better to just ask if it's okay first. Your mom or dad might say, sure, go ahead, if I can't buy you expensive stuff, at least someone can! But there's also the possibility that he or she will warn you that your other parent doesn't really have the money to splurge either, so it wouldn't be nice to try to guilt him or her into it.

Try not to think of budgeting as a punishment but as an opportunity to become more responsible and more financially aware — you know, the whole "money doesn't grow on trees" thing. It may require some sacrifice, or at least some ingenuity—such as joining the library instead of buying books or swapping clothes with friends in between shopping trips. But you might even be able to put away a little money for something great while you're at it.

everyone reacts
differently

Not all parents react in the same way to their new-found freedom. Yours might start hanging out with their friends more often, going out a lot and enjoying a sort of second childhood. It helps them forget about the divorce for a little while and prove that they're not going to let it get the better of them. Or, they might take the opportunity to do things with you that they didn't have time for before. This could bring you closer in all sorts of new ways.

Mom?

—Dad?

Some parents, on the other hand, feel really defeated. They lose all their energy and enthusiasm, and become introverted. Others escape into their work. Still other parents focus all their attention on their children and put their own emotional and social lives on hold. With any of these types of parents, you might suddenly feel responsible for their distress and even guilty when you leave them on their own for, say, a sleepover with friends. Especially if they say things like, "Oh, so I'm going to be on my own tonight, am I? Lucky that there's a good movie on TV." By acting this way, they're making you play a role that you shouldn't have to. It's not your job to replace the absent partner and keep them from being alone. Many parents find it hard to live alone, since they haven't really had to do it much before. They miss having someone around and can't bear the silence. They don't want to go to the movies or to dinner or even for a walk if there's no one to do it with them.

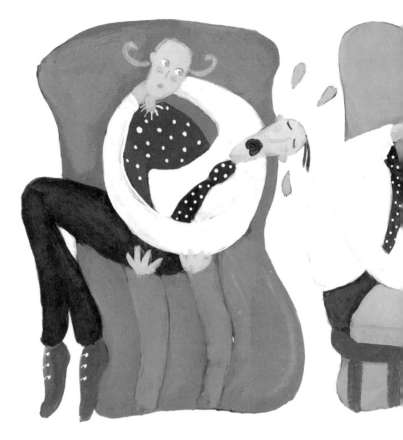

If you're old enough to begin to understand your parents as people and accept them with all their good and bad points, then you're also old enough to take responsibility for your own emotional and psychological health. Part of this is realizing that you don't have to be your parents' new best friend. You're their son or daughter, and even if you're very close, your relationship should still be that of parent and child, not buddy or babysitter or anything else.

Claire's father wasn't handling the departure of his wife very well. He just sat all alone in his apartment getting more and more depressed. Whenever Claire went to his place for the weekend she felt as if she had

to look after a big baby or a little brother. She helped him do the shopping, ironing, and cleaning, and listened to his moaning all night. One
day it all got to be too much for her. "I couldn't take any more. I felt like
his mother, sister, and friend, but never his daughter. I was bogged
down in a situation that was way over my head. I spoke to his best friend
about it and he took over. My dad and I talked about the situation and
now he doesn't go overboard telling me all of his worries anymore.
Everything's much easier now and I'm starting to enjoy my weekends
with him."

the new partner

Say you just learned that your mom has gotten engaged to a new guy. You're probably feeling really frightened. It could be hard to let go of this fear of being replaced—or of having one of your parents replaced—by someone who has nothing to do with your family or your past. Hundreds of questions are probably swirling around in your head. "What will Dad think? Will he be upset? Should I tell him about the new guy?" It's not up to you to sort out these issues—it's the responsibility of the adults involved. But that likely won't stop you from somehow feeling that meeting the new person is disloyal to your father, or betrays his trust. And you don't dare tell your mother what you're thinking: "Is she going to forget me completely and devote herself to this new guy? Will he try to come between me and my mom?" You don't want to cause any problems for her. Still, you remember the stories of Snow White and Cinderella—you know what stepparents are capable of! So maybe you start making evil plans about how to separate them as soon as possible. Maybe you should ignore him, make his life impossible by refusing to do what he asks, and then criticize every word he says. Perhaps you could refuse to eat at the same table as him. Or, maybe you'll give mom the silent treatment till she gets the picture. Or just pretend to be blissfully ignorant about what's going on and prove to the new guy that his arrival

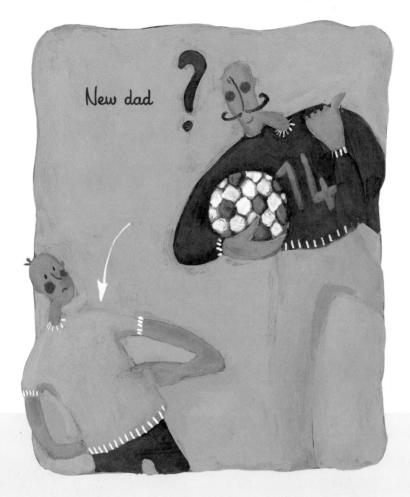

New dad **?**

will make no difference to your life at all. Yeah, that'll show him.

Of course, secretly, you may be happy about this new relationship because it gets your mother off your back and you won't have to listen to her criticize your dad or mope around anymore.

It's true that a new boyfriend or girlfriend can make a lonely parent happier, more relaxed, more sociable, and even more affectionate. And that can be a big relief. There are two people sharing the little daily crises again now. They're close, they talk to each other often, they see friends and go out, giving you time to breathe. This could be a big weight off your shoulders—you can stop worrying about them now.

the first
encounter

It has to happen sometime—you've got to meet this new person who's swept your mom or dad off her or his feet. Let's say it's your dad who's got the new flame. Picture it: you watch her arrive, thinking you would never have chosen someone like that. She's too small, too big, has a silly laugh, or dresses like your grandmother. Nothing about her escapes your attention, none of her little flaws or mannerisms. She seems bossy, which doesn't bode well if there's a chance she's going to be your stepmother. Or, on the other hand, she seems soft and you think you could wind her around your little finger. Or maybe she doesn't bring about any reaction at all in you except mistrust

and you'd rather just ignore the whole thing for the moment. Of course, sometimes, deep down, you approve of your dad's choice. His new girlfriend does seem friendly, funny, and sort of pretty, for an old person. But you're just not ready to admit that right now. There's no way she'll replace your mom in your heart and you want her to know that. But then she must be thinking the same thing, you say to yourself. She can't be expecting to become a replacement mother.

Whatever your feelings, a new person represents an intrusion and yet again, another change. Just try to sympathize with him or her, though. Remember how uncomfortable it must feel to be under the spotlight. It's not any easier for him or her than it is for you. You're wondering what the person thinks about you, and you sort of feel like your mother or father is testing you in some way when they introduce you. The first meeting isn't likely to be natural or relaxed when everyone feels embarrassed, anxious, and scrutinized.

getting to know you

Getting to know each other takes more than one after-
noon. At the beginning you may feel reluctant to even try, afraid that
this person will interfere with your life, just as it finally seemed to be
getting back on track. It's just like when a new kid moves to town—you
look at him with a little bit of suspicion at first because he represents
an unknown future. You're probably wondering if this new relationship is

going to be serious. Will it last or will
you have to go through another
breakup?

But don't get ahead of yourself—there's no rush. You need to take
time to get to know this stranger.
You'll start to connect when you start
spending more time together. As you
do, allow yourself to feel a range of
emotions, both positive and negative,
and that'll make it easier to allow the
new person into your life. Don't just
ignore your negative feelings—
allow yourself to feel angry and sad and even resentful toward your parents. Stifling these emotions might make you take them out on your

mom or dad's new partner—consciously or subconsciously. The adults need to be patient and tolerant, too. If things get tense, talk to your mom or dad. While it's not right for you to be an intermediary between them, they can and should be intermediaries between you and their new partners. At the same time, it's perfectly okay

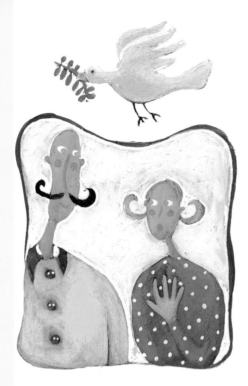

for you to talk to the new partner directly. Staying silent can only make things worse. If you put your concerns into words, you'll feel much better and a little of the tension will be relieved.

When Alexander met his mother's new friend, his first impression was that the guy was a snob. Alexander was used to a relaxed, and, he admits, pretty untidy regime at home and his mom's boyfriend's extreme cleanliness and orderliness came as a sort of culture shock. All his mom and the guy talked about were golf and dinners with important business people until one day Alexander suggested they go out to eat together. They talked about what was on his mind and things were more relaxed after that. "He listened carefully to what I had to say. We have different tastes and ways of looking at stuff, but we managed to talk. Since I live with my dad we don't see each other that much, but now we'll be okay with each other and make a real effort to get along when we do."

coming to grips with the
situation

Whether you feel good or bad about this new partner,
don't worry. Both reactions are totally normal. But even if you wish he or
she didn't have to be around so often, it's important to realize that
many adults need to be close with other adults in order to feel totally
happy. And eventually, they may build a new family together with you
right at heart of it. This really is a good thing, despite the fact that the
arrival of a stepparent may mark the final end to your secret dream of
getting your parents back together. The new partnership may seem to
threaten the close, privileged relation-
ship you've built up with your parent,
but it doesn't
have to.

During the early stages, everyone will keep an eye on each other and try to figure out where they fit into the equation. You don't have to love the new person immediately, but you do have to respect him or her. Respect doesn't mean that you necessarily feel affection for the new partner. It just means that you're granting him or her a place in the family. Obviously, this takes some effort on your part—it takes a really mature kid to realize that a stepparent deserves to be allowed into your little family circle, and that doing this won't affect the closeness you have with your mom or dad.

Caroline was pretty suspicious of Paul when he moved into the apartment she had shared with her mother for five years. She had to move some of her clothes to make room for his, and she had to try not to play her CDs at full blast when he was concentrating on his work. Paul, on the other hand, found it hard to accept that Caroline and her mom spent so much time chatting in the bathroom. There was some friction at the beginning, along with a few awkward exchanges, including the classics, "You are not my father" and "You can't tell me what to do," followed by the inevitable response, "If I were your father, I'd . . . " (you can fill in the rest). After a few weeks of heated discussions, slammed doors, and lots of tissues, all parties learned to pay a little more attention to each other's needs and feelings.

Try to be patient as you get used to the new rhythm of daily family life—it won't always be as weird and awkward as it seems right now. Letting everyone express themselves and then establishing some new house rules—for you and your stepparent to follow—can help.

part of the
new scenery

There's no reason why you can't ask your mother or father to keep some time free for you two to spend together, just the two of you, without your stepparent. You can use the time to reminisce about past events he or she wouldn't find interesting or amusing, for instance, the

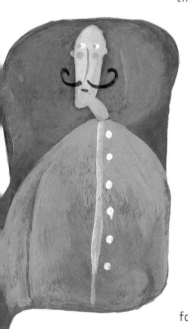

time you all fell on the floor laughing when Aunt Martha lost her teeth during a family dinner. You can use it to sort out any issues at home or in the rest of your life, or you can just enjoy each other's company.

Slowly things will get easier with your stepmother or father. You'll even build up your own history and memories together. If you want to jump-start that part of your relationship, invite him or her to come to one of your dance classes or ask for help you with your homework. Your step-

parent will feel flattered that you want him or her to be part of your life. And feeling like you have some sort of relationship with your stepparent will make those "Clean your room!" or "Have you set the table?" moments more bearable.

am i still part of this
new family?

Love doesn't depend on courts or documents. The law doesn't grant your parent's new spouse any right to make important decisions about your life. You're not blood relatives, and he or she has no legal obligation to feed, house, or educate you. By the same token, you have no responsibilities toward him or her. In the eyes of the law, you might as well be strangers to each other. What brings you together is your love for the same person—your mom or dad. A new marriage only ties the two adults involved together, not their children. You won't take his name or inherit her assets unless you're legally adopted.

However, you'll still be a son or daughter in the new family context, and the stepparent will still be a parent. You need to respect each other in this relationship and be aware that it's based on a marriage—a union with your mother or father, whom he or she loves. Your stepparent didn't start off as your friend, but could turn into one. Or, the two of you could stay strictly parent/child. It's up to both of you how much of an emotional impact this relationship has on you.

new experiences,
new ties

So now you have two families—a biological one and a household one. You have different last names and different backgrounds but you're going to create a new world together, with new emotional ties. More and more families are stepfamilies today. And there are no set rules of behavior that govern all of them. The relationship between stepparent and stepchild could be described as a sort of pact or agreement between people who didn't choose each other but were thrown together by life.

If both your parents remarry, you'll have to get used to two new homes, both of which could be very different from each other in terms of how the family members act toward each other and what's expected of them. So what are you supposed to do if the rules in your original household were totally different from those in the two new ones? For example, say at your mother's house you don't have to sit down for dinner and everyone eats wherever and whenever they want. But it's exactly the opposite at your father's place, where you're expected to be ready at a certain time to sit down and all eat together. While it may seem confusing and, frankly, a little annoying—and make you wonder how good these rules can be if only one of your parents believes in them anyway—it's actually not all that complicated. Think of it as being like school: each of your classes is different, so you follow the English teacher's rules in English, and the math teacher's rules in math. To make things even clearer, it's important to establish the new rules within each family as early as possible. Do you have to do what your new stepparent says? The answer is yes, once the different rules and regulations have been established and agreed upon. And, unless your family has made an agreement to the contrary, if you don't follow the rules, your stepparent has the right to punish you just as your mom or dad would if you disobeyed them.

names and last names

There's no law governing your relationship with your step-parent, and no great name to call him or her, either. "Hi Step-Dad!" doesn't have much of a ring to it. And everyone remembers the stepmothers of fairy tales—they're always the witches who try to make their stepchildren's lives miserable! But he's not actually your father and she's not actually your mother, so "Hi, Dad" or "Hi, Mom" isn't right, either.

Wicked stepmother

Most kids call their stepparents by their first names, although some psychologists wonder if this makes the relationship between generations more confusing. Usually people of the same generation—that is, people who are around the same age—use each other's first names, and young people call those older than them Mr. or Mrs. But that seems way too formal a way to address someone who's a part of your family and may even be living with you. In the absence of any better way of handling the situation, first names are the answer. But of course, you're free to come up with alternatives or think up other names that only you use. Whatever suits you best.

and he has kids, too!

You may already have brothers and sisters, but what if your new stepparent arrives with his or her own children in tow? Even if you're about the same age, you probably haven't been brought up in exactly the same way and haven't had the same experiences. It's not uncommon to feel threatened by these newcomers or consider them new allies against the adults.

Whichever way you feel, it's yet another upheaval for you to cope with. You'll need to get used to the kids, just the way you got used to their mom or dad, and you may have to learn to live under the same roof. Just as nobody expected you to love your parent's new spouse at

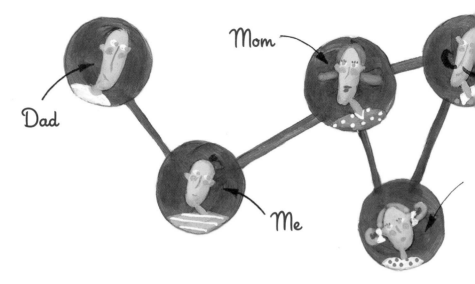

Dad

Mom

Me

first sight, you're not expected to love your new stepbrothers and step-sisters immediately, either. They're not your "real" brothers and sisters and you have the right to feel a certain degree of animosity toward them. They're squeezing into a place that you may not have felt like sharing. In a legal context, you have no attachment to them. So the relationship you're most likely to form with them is that of friends. Depending on their ages, you may suddenly lose your position as the oldest or the youngest child, and that's another thing you'll have to deal with: you'll have to find your place in the new family structure.

So how do you introduce them to your friends? You probably call them stepsisters and stepbrothers. But if you get along well together, why not just call them brother and sister? It would be a really warm and welcoming gesture, and could cement the positive relationship you've already got going. But if you're still hesitant and getting to know each

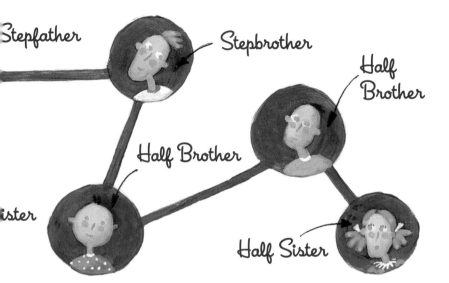

Stepfather

Stepbrother

Half Brother

Half Brother

ister

Half Sister

other, don't get too informal by dropping the "step" just yet—if they're not ready for it, it might make them feel uncomfortable, like you're forcing them to be friendlier than they want to be.

You may be obligated to share your bedroom with some annoying little runt who likes awful music and leaves her clothes all over the floor. Or some intimidating older kid who thinks your music is awful and yells at *you* for the clothes on the floor. You could try dividing the room into two separate areas (minus the big, melodramatic strip of black tape you see on TV) or working out your differences to create a space in which you both feel comfortable. Just like you did with your stepparent, establish some roommate rules between yourselves, and make sure you're both willing to respect them. Try to do it on your own without involving the adults unless you really can't come to an agreement.

another new arrival

It's natural for many new couples to want to have a baby. This might make you feel sort of anxious—afraid that a new arrival could take the place in the family that you're already finding difficult to share with the other kids. Maybe you also thought you noticed your father make a face when your mother told him she was pregnant. If his own life isn't quite as settled as your mom's yet, he may be a little jealous, or worried that you'll become more and more attached to your new family because of the new baby. This happened to Anna, whose mother

arranged for her to see less and less of her father once his new wife got pregnant. There was always something else that she wanted Anna to do —shopping, seeing the dentist, visiting Grandma. She was terrified of losing Anna. But Anna was dying to see the new baby. She finally had to lie and say she was going to a friend's house when she was really going to her dad's. When she got back, Anna showed her mom the photos of the baby. That's when she realized how much this birth meant to her daughter.

It was a similar situation, but the opposite, with Ben. Trying to protect his father who lived alone, he told his mother not to tell his dad that she was having a baby. "I was really scared about how he would react. I was sure he would be hurt. But then Mom started to show, and Dad wound up chewing her out for hiding the pregnancy from him. In the end, though, he reacted really well. He was happy for me that I was getting a new stepbrother or sister, and he reassured me that he'd get his own life back together soon."

future family

Even if you're not aware of it, observing your own family has taught you about what being a couple entails. So, since your mom and dad's marriage didn't work out, you might be wondering if your dream of falling in love, getting married, and growing old together with your husband or wife is nothing but an illusion. Especially with the great example your parents set for you! What's the point of getting married if all it leads to is fighting and divorce? The truth is, it doesn't have to be this way. Right now, many couples find a way out of their problems through divorce. But in the future, things might not be the same. You and your generation can learn from your parents' mistakes, instead of repeating them. You won't follow in their footsteps as long as you remember that you are not them—you are your own person, and you'll do things your way. In fact, even though you don't have full knowledge of

ties

what really went on between your parents, experiencing their divorce will, with luck, give you at least a little bit of insight as to what works and what doesn't in relationships. In your own life, you'll experience good things and bad things, pitfalls and challenges. Getting together and breaking up with girlfriends or boyfriends will help you figure out how to handle the ups and downs of relationships. With all you've been through, you have learned to be flexible, and to adapt to different people and different situations—and you can carry that with you throughout your life. All of the different people and environments you'll have grown up with—your mother and father together at first, then each separately, then with stepparents, if you have them—offer you something to learn from. It's up to you to pick out what's best from everything you've seen, and to make the best life for yourself going forward.

Bibliography

Hotlines
The National Child Abuse Hotline
1-800-422-4453

The National Domestic Violence Hotlines
1-800-799-7233 or 1-800-787-3244

Books
Fox, Paula. *Monkey Island.* New York: Orchard Books, 1991.

Gripe, Maria. *La fille de papa Pèlerine (The Daughter of Father Pèlerine),* Folio Junior. Paris: Gallimard-Jeunesse, 1994.

Kästner, Erich. *Deux pour une (Two for One),* Le Livre de Poche. Paris: Hachette Jeunesse, 2001.

Lucet, Michel. *Divisé par deux (Divided by Two),* Page Blanche. Paris: Gallimard-Jeunesse, 1988.

Modiano, Patrick. *Catherine Certitude,* Folio Junior. Paris: Gallimard-Jeunesse, 1988.

Murail, Marie-Aude. *Nos amours ne vont pas si mal (Our Love isn't going so badly),* Médium. L'École des loisirs, 1995.

Tasma, Sophie. *Emma,* Medium. L'École des loisirs, 1995.

Winberg, Anna Greta, *Ce jeudi d'octobre (This Thursday in October).* Le Livre de Poche. Paris: Hachette Jeunesse, 2002.

Web sites
The Better Divorce Network
www.betterdivorce.com

National Center for Health Statistics
www.cdc.gov/nchs

Frequently Asked Questions About Divorce
www.broomfieldlaw.com/divorce-faq.htm

Divorce magazine
www.divorcemag.com

Ontario Consultants on Religious Tolerance
www.religioustolerance.org

Smart Marriages
www.smartmarriages.com

Index